PATCHWORK &
QUILTING

PATCHWORK & QUILTING

Master new sewing skills with these
simple-to-make projects

KATHARINE GUERRIER

CHARTWELL
BOOKS, INC.

A QUINTET BOOK

Published by Chartwell Books
A Division of Book Sales, Inc.
114 Northfield Avenue
Edison, New Jersey 08837

This edition produced for sale in the U.S.A., its
territories and dependencies only.

ISBN 0-7858-0363-7

This book was designed and produced by
Quintet Publishing Limited
6 Blundell Street
London N7 9BH

Creative Director: Richard Dewing
Designer: Isobel Gillan
Project Editor: Diana Steedman
Editor: Lydia Darbyshire
Illustrator: Elsa Godfrey
Photographer: Andrew Sydenham

Typeset in Great Britain by
Central Southern Typesetters, Eastbourne
Manufactured by Eray Scan Pte. Ltd., Singapore
Printed by Star Standard Industries (Pte.) Ltd., Singapore

ACKNOWLEDGMENTS
All items designed by Katharine Guerrier.
Corded cushion made by Lynn Cooke,
all other items made by Katharine Guerrier.

Many thanks to my husband George Hudson for practical
support and help in this and previous publications.

The Publishers are grateful to The Quilt Room,
20 West Street, Dorking, Surrey for their advice and help with
materials and equipment.

CONTENTS

INTRODUCTION 6

THE PROJECTS

Picnic or Play Quilt 10

Housewarming Floor Pillow 12

Corded and Quilted Pillow 16

Star and Pinwheel Shoulder Bag 19

Curtain Tieback 22

Christmas Table Mats 24

Fan Motif Pincushion and Needlecase 27

"Quillow" or Lap Quilt 30

Flying Geese Storage Tube 34

Wall Pockets 37

Belt or Shoulder Purse 40

Crazy Patchwork Wall Hanging 42

TEMPLATES 45

INTRODUCTION

In these twelve easy projects, some of the popular traditional patchworks, such as "Flying Geese," "Checkerboard," and "Houses," are designed to introduce you to this fascinating craft and tempt you to create useful items for your home, or for your family and friends.

Both patchwork and quilting are crafts with a long-standing tradition, closely linked with social history and still enjoyed for their unique combination of functional, decorative, and creative elements. Some of the items featured are easy enough for a child or a complete beginner to attempt, such as the Play Quilt or the Fan Motif Pincushion and Needlecase set, while others present more of a challenge, like the Corded Pillow or the Curtain Tieback. A "Quillow" and a floor pillow are also featured, along with other ideas for gifts or to decorate your home.

Before you begin, read the following section, which outlines the basics of making patchwork and of quilting. Then each of the twelve projects has clear illustrations and instructions to help you achieve perfect results. The back pages provide all the templates you will need and lists cutting out details for each project.

MATERIALS

As a general rule, pure cotton dress-weight fabrics are best to start with. These are easier to handle and will press well. A visit to a fabric store will demonstrate the wide choice of fabrics available in all sorts of designs: floral, geometric, novelty, plaids and stripes, large and small prints, as well as a large number of solid colors. Aim to include dark, medium, and light shades in your selection – many experienced quilters choose fabrics in the same way an artist selects paints, by building up a wide palette from which to choose when making quilts and other items. Patchwork suppliers are happy to cut small pieces, and many put together packs of harmonizing fabrics for the beginner.

Before starting a project, wash all fabrics to remove any residual dressing and dye, and cut off the selvages.

EQUIPMENT

In order to begin patchwork, you will need a basic sewing kit and a few drawing and measuring tools. Although there is a vast array of specialist tools available for quilters, it is better to start simply with what you already have in the home and add to your equipment as it becomes necessary and your skills increase.

The following is all you will need to make a start:

- dressmaking scissors
- a small pair of embroidery scissors or thread snips
- needles and pins
- sewing machine if desired
- threads for basting and to match fabrics
- tape measure
- thimble
- seam ripper

For drawing and measuring:

- ruler
- pencils and eraser
- good-quality paper
- tracing paper
- cardboard or template plastic
- pencil sharpener
- craft knife or paper scissors
- colored pencils and graph paper will help with the design process

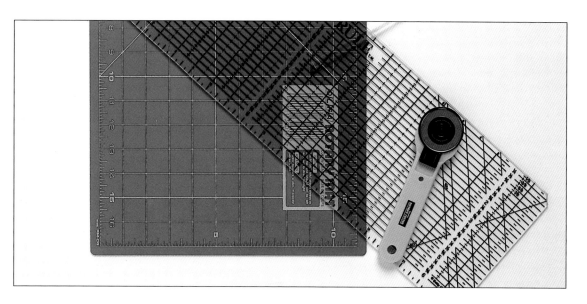

Rotary cutting set

Many of the simple shapes in patchwork can be easily cut without templates, using a rotary cutting set. A certain amount of practice is needed to learn how to use the cutter effectively, but once mastered it can reduce the time spent cutting out fabrics by more than half.

The basic rotary cutting equipment consists of a self-healing cutting board, the rotary ruler, and the cutter itself. Different sizes are available in all these pieces, but a good set to begin with would be a board 17 x 23 inches, a ruler 6 x 24 inches, and the large size cutter.

The sharp circular blade on the cutter is protected by a guard – get into the habit of putting the guard on each time you put the cutter down and always cut away from your body. A new blade can cut through up to eight layers of fabric and should last well if care is taken to protect it.

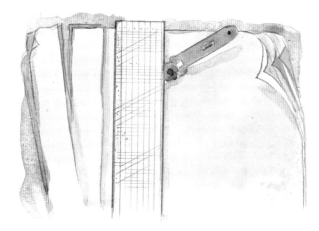

Using the grid on the rotary ruler – align the appropriate line on the ruler with the edge of the fabric and cut.

The board and the ruler are both marked with a grid, and the ruler has a non-beveled edge to stop the blade from slipping across when in use. Never use a rotary cutter with a flat or beveled ruler as this could be dangerous.

Prepare the fabric for cutting out patches by first straightening and squaring the crosswise grain (selvage to selvage across the width) as follows: fold the fabric in half with selvages together, then fold again, placing the second fold in line with the selvage edges. Smooth the layers together and steam press, then place the fabric on the board. Position the ruler on the fabric with one of the horizontal grid lines level with the double fold, which should be at the front of the board. Slide the ruler to the edge of the fabric, then hold it firmly down while you push the cutter along the edge of the ruler to trim and straighten the edges of the fabric. By creating a 90-degree angle in the fabric as you cut, aligning a horizontal line on the ruler with the folded

edges and the vertical edge of the ruler on the edges to be cut, you will ensure that the strips of fabric will not be distorted or form a "V" shape. When the edge has been straightened, fabric can be cut into strips, squares, rectangles, and triangles by using either the grid on the board or on the ruler.

To use the grid on the board, place the fabric in line with both horizontal and vertical grid lines and cut the required sizes by lining up the ruler with the measurements on the board. To use the grid on the ruler, line up the appropriate line on the ruler with the cut edge of the fabric, thus holding the fabric under the ruler, and cut. The bulk of the fabric should be on the right if you are right-handed, and on the left if you are left-handed.

Once strips are cut, they can be subcut into squares and rectangles. To cut half-square triangles, first cut squares, then divide them across from corner to corner.

BASIC TECHNIQUES

Most of the projects in this book are self-explanatory, but a few basic techniques are a useful foundation to build on. It is important to realize that accuracy is necessary in all stages of patchwork, from making the templates through to cutting out the fabrics and stitching the patches together.

Making templates

Trace or draw the template using the measurements given and transfer to a firm material such as cardboard or template plastic. The seam allowance used in patchwork is ¼ inch, and this can be added to the template or to the fabric as you cut out the patches. Templates given in this book have a sewing line (dotted) and a cutting line (solid).

Usually, templates for *hand* piecing are the finished size of the patch, i.e. no seam allowance, and templates for *machine* piecing have seam allowance added.

Marking and cutting the fabrics

Place the template on the wrong side of the fabric, aligning the straight grain correctly and mark around the outer edges. For hand piecing, this line is your sewing guideline. Add a seam allowance as you cut the fabric. Remember to leave a large enough gap between the patches to accommodate the seam allowances.

For machine piecing, cut on the line as the template already has the seam allowance added. Patches can therefore be marked edge to edge on the fabric.

Sewing the patches together

Patches are placed right sides together and stitched with a running stitch by hand or machine. When hand piecing, use small stitches with an occasional backstitch to strengthen the seam. Begin and end the seam with two or three backstitches and sew on the marked lines. When machine stitching seams, position the presser foot to give the correct seam allowance and guide the fabrics through the machine right

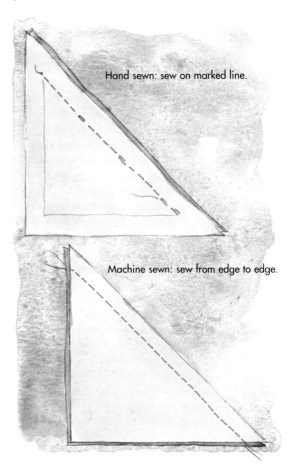

Hand sewn: sew on marked line.

Machine sewn: sew from edge to edge.

across from edge to edge. Press seams to one side; the darker side if possible. Where several seams come together, press the final seam open to avoid bulk.

Building up the patchwork

Start with the smaller patches and stitch in straight lines wherever possible. All projects have piecing order diagrams and follow logical sequences. When experimenting with new blocks, study the diagrams to work out the best way to build up the design.

FINISHING TECHNIQUES

Finishing techniques for most of the projects are included with the instructions, so this section will deal only with one or two which are common to several items.

Quilting

Quilting serves the dual purpose of fastening the layers of the quilt together and forming a decorative texture on the surface. It is done with a running stitch, traditionally by hand, but machine quilting is gaining in popularity as it is so much quicker. The layers of the quilted item – the top, the batting, and the backing fabric must be fastened together so that the layers will not shift, either with a grid of basting stitches or safety pins placed at regular intervals. Quilt from the center out if possible and try to keep your stitches as even as possible. To begin and end each length of thread, tie a knot and pop it through into the middle layer of the quilt "sandwich" to keep the work looking neat on the front and back.

Making a fabric loop

Cut a strip of fabric the required length and width. Fold in half lengthwise, right sides together, and stitch along the long edge. Press the seam open and into the center of the back, then stitch across one short end. Turn the loop through to the right side with a blunt ended knitting needle and press again. Trim loop to required length.

Binding

For items which need to be bound, cut binding strips from coordinating fabric to match the patchwork, between 2–2½ inches wide according to the project, and use double for more durability. Fold the strips right side out and place the side with raw edges along the top side of the quilt. Stitch through all layers. The folded edge can then be hemmed down onto the back of the quilt, enclosing all raw edges. For a quick machine binding, stitch the binding along the edges of the quilt on the *wrong* side, then fold over to the right side of the quilt and machine stitch along the folded edge.

Finish the short ends at the corners neatly or with a folded miter.

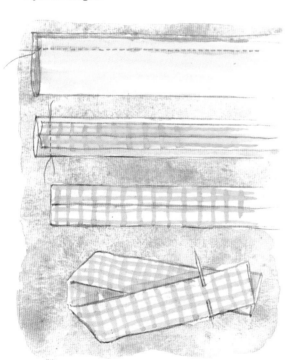

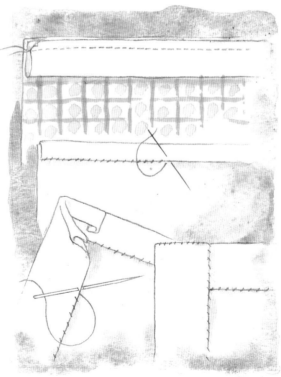

PICNIC OR PLAY QUILT

Finished size: 41 x 41 inches

Suitable for a picnic or for a baby's play *pen, this practical quilt is an ideal project for someone who is just beginning to work with patchwork. It can be quickly made from squares and rectangles, and the quilting, which is in straight lines, can be done by hand or by machine.*

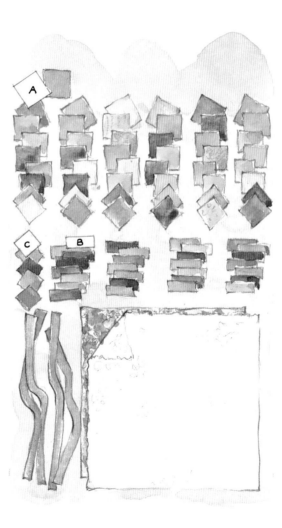

YOU WILL NEED

- needle, threads to match, pins, scissors
- patterned fabrics: a total of 1½ yards scrap fabrics, pieces larger than 5½ inches square
- solid fabrics: ½ yard in pieces larger than 5½ x 3½ inches
- backing fabric: 1½ yards
- lightweight polyester batting: 45 x 45 inches
- coordinated fabric for binding: ½ yard

1 Trace and make templates shown on page 45 from cardboard or plastic. Follow cutting instructions on page 45.

2 Taking ¼-inch seam allowances, piece the squares together in rows of seven, alternating the fabrics to achieve a checkerboard effect. Press seams toward the darker fabric. Stitch the rows together, making sure the seams align. Press long seams to one side. Then join the rectangles in four sets of seven to make borders. Add a corner square to each end of two of these.

3 **Adding the borders.** Stitch the borders to the sides of the quilt, with the long strips on two opposite sides of the patchwork.

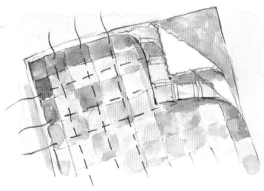

4 **Quilting.** Place the backing fabric, wrong side up, on a flat surface and place the batting on top. Place the finished patchwork right side up in the center. Pin, then baste the three layers together, making rows of stitches both horizontally and vertically about 4 inches apart. Quilt by hand or machine, using the seams as a guide. Trim the backing and batting even with the patchwork.

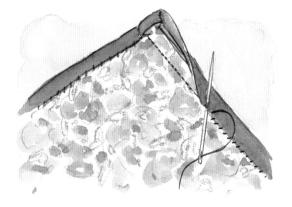

5 Complete the quilt by binding the raw edges. For a quick machine binding, or hand stitched binding, see the technique explained on page 9.

11

HOUSEWARMING FLOOR PILLOW

Finished size: 36 x 36 inches

A *simple pictorial block is repeated four times in the center of the pillow, which has multiple borders, some with corner squares. We have made it in plaids and striped fabrics, which give it a homey appearance. The front of the pillow cover is machine pieced for strength and machine quilted, but if preferred, it could be hand quilted.*

1 Trace and make templates on page 45 from cardboard or plastic. Follow cutting instructions listed on page 45. Cut out the pieces accurately. Do not cut the borders until you have finished stitching the blocks so you can be sure the lengths fit.

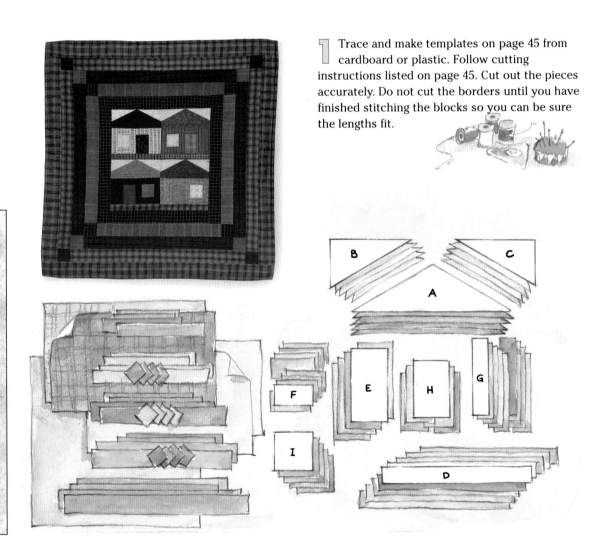

YOU WILL NEED

- needle, threads to match, pins, scissors
- cardboard for templates
- colored fabrics (six shades for each block): 9 x 36 inches (in total for each block); 1 yard for the borders; 1¾ yards for the outer border and back
- lightweight polyester batting: 40 x 40 inches
- lining for back of cover: 1½ yards
- zipper: 35 inches long
- pillow form: 36 x 36 inches

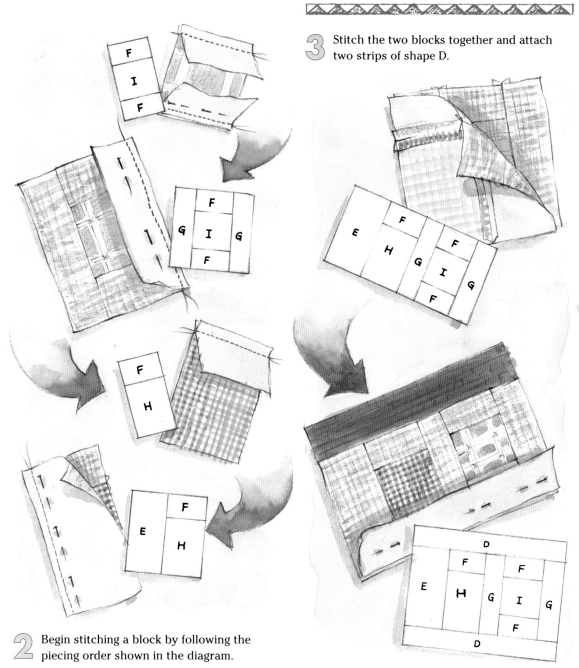

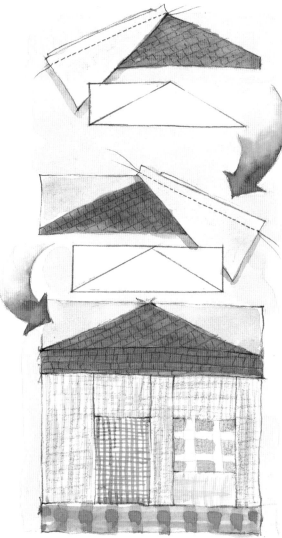

3 Stitch the two blocks together and attach two strips of shape D.

2 Begin stitching a block by following the piecing order shown in the diagram.

4 Piece the roofing shapes together to complete the block. Stitch four blocks in all, putting the window and door in opposite sides in two of the blocks to give variety. When you have stitched all four blocks, assemble them into a large block.

5 **Adding the borders.** Cut two strips 2½ x 16½ inches (check the length before cutting) and stitch them in place at the top and bottom of the center panel. Cut two more strips, 2½ x 20½ inches, for the sides, again checking length before cutting.

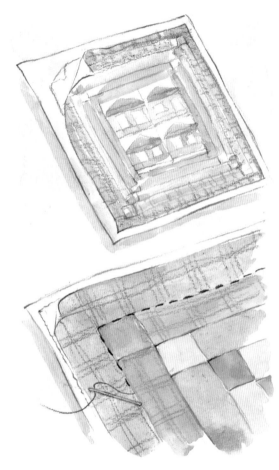

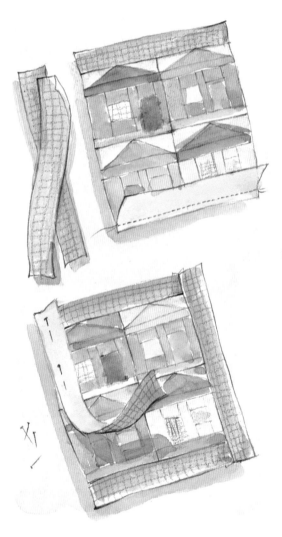

6 Cut four strips the length of the sides and 2½ inches wide. Cut four 2½-inch squares in contrasting fabric for the corners. Make the third and fourth borders in the same way, joining strips if necessary to make the strips long enough.

7 The fifth border is cut from the material used for the back of the pillow. Cut strips 3¼ inches wide and stitch them as for the first border (i.e. top and bottom first, then running right up the sides).

8 **Quilting.** Cut a square of backing fabric 1 inch larger all around than the finished patchwork and lay it, right side down, on a flat surface. Place the batting on top and the patchwork, right side up, on top. Smooth carefully, then pin and baste the layers together, stitching vertically and horizontally in rows about 4 inches apart to form a grid. Quilt by machine or hand, following the contours of the patchwork.

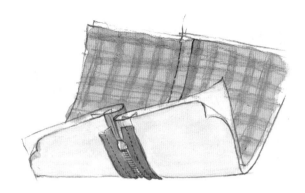

9 From the remaining fabric for the back, cut two pieces, each 22 x 39 inches. Cut two pieces the same size from the lining fabric. Place together right sides facing, and stitch along one long edge, with ¼-inch seam allowances. Turn right side out and press a new fold in the fabric so that the seam lies 1½ inches from the new edge. Repeat with the other two pieces. Insert the zipper between the two sections of the back, concealing it by overlapping one back section by 1 inch.

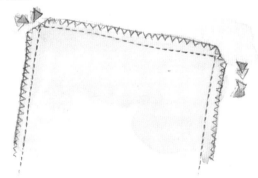

10 Place the pillow front and back pieces together, right sides facing, and smooth carefully. Pin and baste together, then, with the patchwork on top, stitch around the edge, taking a seam allowance of ¼ inch. Trim the seams and corners, then overcast all seams before turning right side out. Insert the pillow form.

CORDED AND QUILTED PILLOW

Finished size: 14 x 14 inches

The leaf motif on this pillow cover was achieved by a technique known as Italian quilting or corded quilting, which is ideal for linear patterns. The raised effect is achieved by threading quilting wool through stitched channels, and we have enhanced the simple corded design by additional quilting.

1 Trace and make the templates shown on page 45. Follow the cutting instructions listed on page 45. Note the cut on the bias.

YOU WILL NEED

- needle, threads to match, pins, scissors
- cream fabric: 27 x 36 inches
- cardboard or plastic for templates
- gauze or loosely woven fabric: 27 x 36 inches
- dressmaker's chalk
- quilting wool and large tapestry needle
- lightweight polyester batting: 16 x 16 inches
- lining fabric or gauze: 16 x 16 inches
- quilting thread
- masking tape: ½-inch wide
- zipper: 12 inches long
- pillow form: 12 x 12 inches

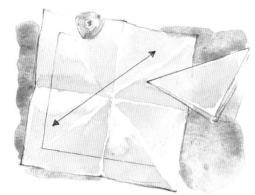

2 Cut the 16 x 16-inch square on the bias of the cream fabric for the front of the pillow. Press to mark the vertical and horizontal mid-lines. Fold in half and half again across the diagonals and press lightly to mark the corner to corner lines. Draw a 12 x 12-inch square as an outer guideline.

3 Position the larger template so that a horizontal line passes through the points of the leaf. The end marked with X should be toward the center. Transfer the outline to the fabric. Repeat on the opposite side and on the two vertical lines and on the two diagonal lines.

4 Use the smaller template to draw lines inside the large leaf shapes.

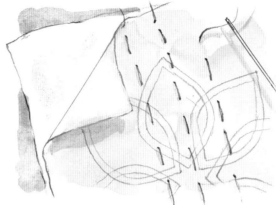

5 Baste the gauze to the back of the pillow front, taking lines of stitches horizontally and vertically across the pillow to make a grid.

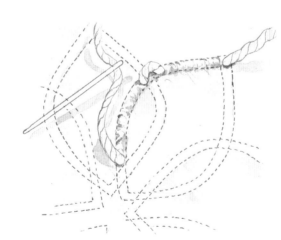

6 Stitch along the marked outlines of the leaf with a small, even running stitch. Where the lines intersect, pass the needle under the back of the diagonal leaves.

7 Beginning with the diagonal leaves, thread a tapestry needle with quilting wool. Push the needle through the gauze into the back of a stitched channel, at one of the points of a leaf. Slide the needle along the channel as far as you can, then bring it out through the gauze.
Pull the wool through the channel so that an end of ¼ inch is left, then reinsert the needle through the same opening and continue, leaving a small loop so that the fabric does not pucker.
Bring the wool out of the starting point and cut it off. Stitch the two ends together to prevent them from slipping through the channel. Work the other three diagonal shapes in the same way.

8 Then work the horizontal and vertical leaves. Where the lines intersect, bring the wool out of the channel and reinsert on the other side of the line.

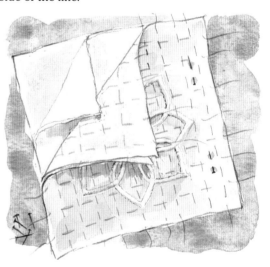

9 Place a square of lining or gauze, 16 x 16 inches, the batting and pillow front in layers and pin and baste together.

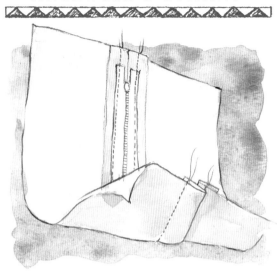

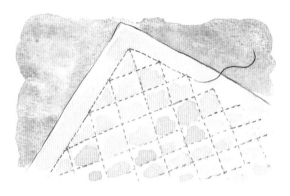

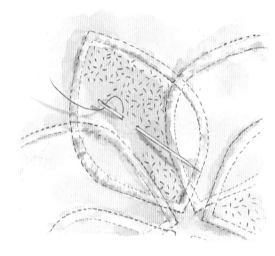

14 Stitch around the outer edge, through all thicknesses, on the 12-inch square line marked in step 2, to form a border. Insert the pillow form.

10 Stipple quilt (small random stitches as illustrated) in the outer vertical and horizontal leaf shapes and in the central area.

12 Cut two pieces of cream fabric, each 16 x 19 inches, for the back of the pillow. Insert the zipper.

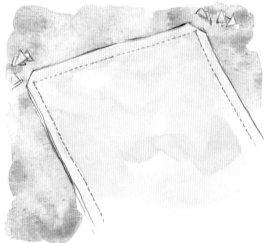

11 Use masking tape to mark a diagonal grid of quilting lines and quilt as illustrated. Trim the pillow front to 15 x 15 inches.

13 Place the front and back right sides together and stitch around all outer edges. Trim the seams and corners and turn right side out.

STAR AND PINWHEEL SHOULDER BAG

Finished size: 16 x 16 inches

We have used four Friendship Star blocks arranged around a central pinwheel for this decorative shoulder bag, which is large enough to hold all the bits and pieces you need.

YOU WILL NEED

- needle, threads to match, pins, scissors
- template plastic or cardboard
- white fabric: 18 x 36 inches
- blue fabric: 27 x 36 inches
- red fabric: 8 x 8 inches
- lightweight polyester batting: 18 x 38 inches
- lining fabric: 18 x 38 inches
- 1 button

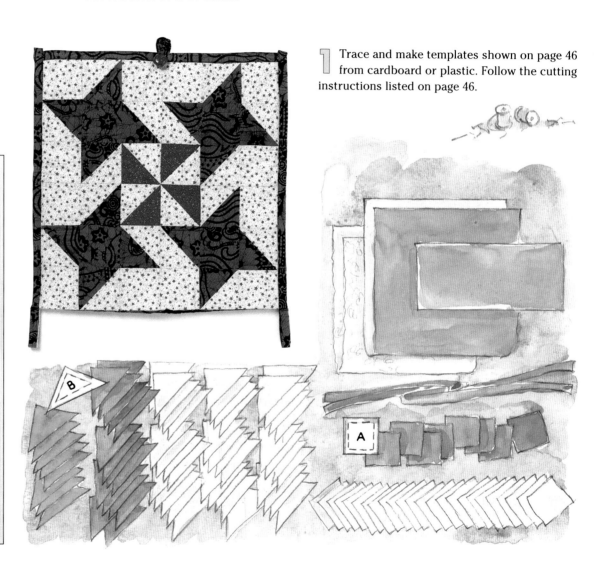

1 Trace and make templates shown on page 46 from cardboard or plastic. Follow the cutting instructions listed on page 46.

3 Stitch the blue fabric strip between the two blocks to form the gusset at the base.

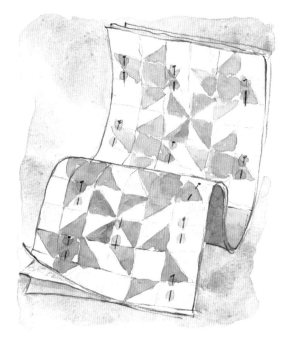

4 Place the lining fabric wrong side up. Lay the batting on it and place the patchwork, right side up on the batting to form a sandwich. Pin and baste the three layers together, making sure you have lines of stitches at intervals of 4 inches, both horizontally and vertically.

2 Follow the piecing diagram above to assemble eight blocks and join these into two blocks of four as shown. Use a seam allowance of ¼ inch on all patchwork pieces.

5 Quilt by hand or machine, using the seams between the patchwork pieces as a guide. Trim the lining and batting so they are level with the patchwork edges.

6 Cut two strips of blue fabric, 2½ x 15½ inches, and fold them in half lengthwise with wrong sides facing. Press. Make a straight binding to cover both short edges of the bag (see page 9).

7 Make a fabric loop through which the button will pass. Insert the loop halfway along one side, under the edge binding.

8 With the patchwork outward and the top edges together, pin and baste the sides of the bag together, folding the gusset in half so that it lies inside the bag. Stitch the sides of the bag together through all thicknesses of fabric.

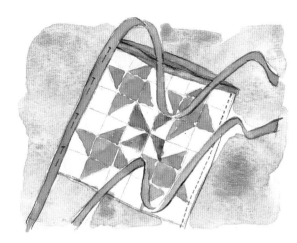

9 Make two more lengths of folded binding for the straps, 2½ x 44 inches, and stitch them to the sides of the bag, extending the line of stitches along the whole length of each strip.

10 Leave 5 inches extending at the bottom on each side and fold these pieces up to form decorative loops at the base of the bag. Knot the straps together so that the bag hangs at a comfortable length and attach the button to the center of the front edge.

CURTAIN TIEBACK

Finished size: 3 x 30 inches

This is a neat way of tying back curtains, and you can select colors that contrast with or are the same shade as the curtains themselves. The checked effect looks complicated, but although it requires some patience, the technique is surprisingly simple.

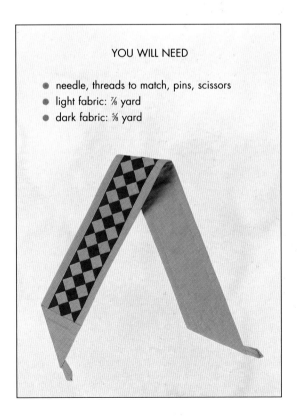

YOU WILL NEED

● needle, threads to match, pins, scissors
● light fabric: ⅞ yard
● dark fabric: ⅝ yard

1 Cutting from selvage to selvage, cut 2 dark strips 1½ inches wide and 2 light and 1 dark strip 1¼ inches wide.

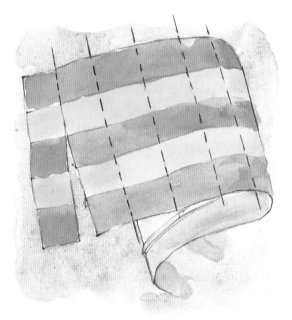

2 Taking a ¼-inch seam allowance, attach the strips in the sequence shown. Press seams toward darker fabric.

Cut the piece across into 26 strips, each 1¼ inches wide. Reposition so that dark and light shades are offset by one strip. Sew strips together, taking care to match the seams. Press the seams on the back.

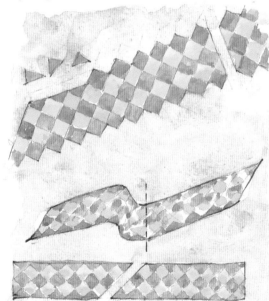

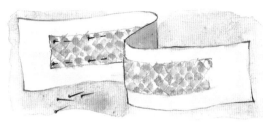

3 Lay the strip flat and mark a vertical line halfway. Cut along the vertical line and reverse the two pieces so that the vertical cuts are at each end and the original end pieces are now adjacent in the center. Stitch these two strips together.

5 Cut a rectangle of light fabric 6 inches wide and 7 inches longer than the patchwork. Place the patchwork exactly in the center, wrong sides together. Pin and baste.

7 At the short end, fold the excess back at an angle of 45 degrees to the bottom edge. Trim and tuck all raw edges neatly inside. Insert a narrow loop, about 4 inches, in each corner at each end and overcast. Reinforce the loops by stitching twice over the corners.

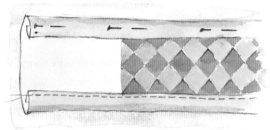

6 On the two long sides, take a double fold to bring the backing over to the right side of the patchwork, so that the edge of the fold is exactly on the corners of the squares in the outer rows. Stitch through the folded edges and the patchwork to hold the turned edge down.

4 Trim the triangles from the edges, leaving ¼ inch beyond the corners of the outer rows of squares.

CHRISTMAS TABLE MATS

Finished size of each mat: 15 x 12 inches

Give your Christmas table setting a festive look with these practical mats. You can either stitch the patchwork by hand, with a running stitch, or machine stitch the pieces together. Similarly, the quilting stitches holding the patchwork, batting, and back together, can be worked by hand or by machine.

YOU WILL NEED FOR FOUR MATS

- needle, threads to match, pins, scissors
- cardboard or plastic for templates
- three patterned fabrics: ⅜ yard of each
- backing fabric: ½ yard
- lightweight batting: 4 pieces, each 14 x 17 inches

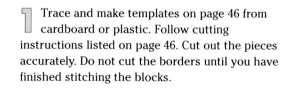

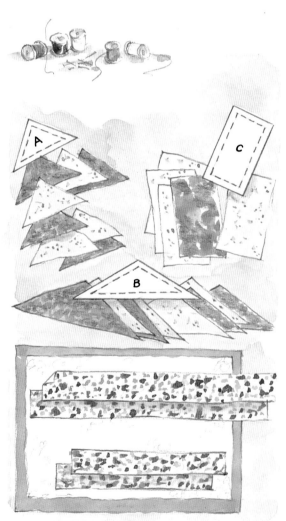

1 Trace and make templates on page 46 from cardboard or plastic. Follow cutting instructions listed on page 46. Cut out the pieces accurately. Do not cut the borders until you have finished stitching the blocks.

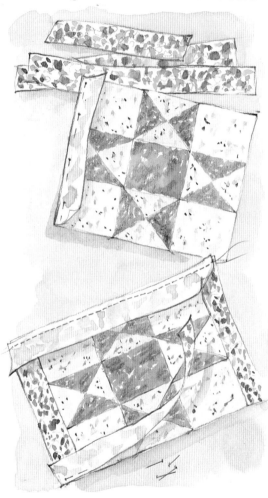

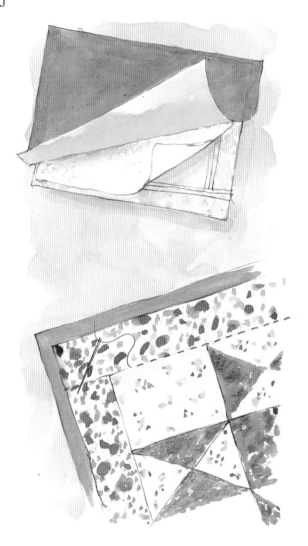

2 Make star points by piecing A and B as shown. Match the center lines. Arrange the rectangles with C pieces and stitch together in three columns. Complete the block by stitching the two long seams. Press well front and back.

3 **Adding the borders.** Stitch the two short borders on first. Add the longer borders to the top and bottom edges and press.

4 **Quilting.** Trim the batting to the exact size of the patchwork and place it on the backing piece. Cut it 1 inch larger all around. Place the patchwork on top. Smooth carefully, then pin and baste before quilting by hand or machine, following the contours of the patchwork.

5 Bring the backing fabric over to the right side of the mat by folding it double and enclosing the raw edges. At the corners, fold the backing so that the point just touches the corner. Trim off the small triangle along the crease, then double-fold around the corner, making a neat miter. Hand or machine hem the edge of the backing to form a neat self-binding.

FAN MOTIF PINCUSHION AND NEEDLECASE

Finished size: 4 inches

The motif for the pincushion and needlecase is made by the paper-piecing method. Each fabric patch is basted to a piece of paper before the patches are stitched together, and when you are working with geometric shapes such as hexagons and diamonds, or with the sections of a motif such as this fan, this method is a good way of making sure that the pieces fit accurately together.

YOU WILL NEED

- needle, threads to match, pins, scissors
- cardboard or plastic for templates
- heavy paper
- scraps of patterned fabric (3 colors)
- solid fabric: 5 x 20 inches
- small quantity polyester stuffing (for pincushion)
- lining fabric: 4½ x 10 inches (for needlecase)
- felt: 2 pieces, each 3¾ inches (for needlecase)
- embroidery thread

1 Trace and make the templates on page 47 from cardboard or plastic. Draw around the templates onto heavy paper. *For each item* cut four fan sections and one corner piece.

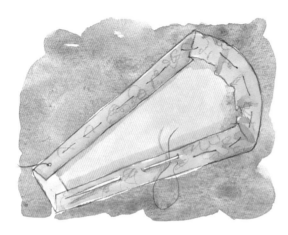

2 **To make the motif:** Pin the five paper sections to the wrong side of the pattern fabric and cut each one out, adding ¼ inch all around for turning. Baste the paper to the fabric, except at the narrow ends of the fan pieces and the two straight edges of the corner piece.

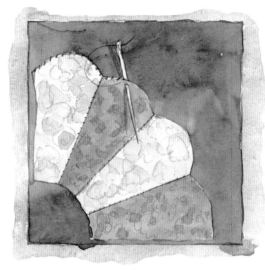

4 Apply interfacing to the 4½-inch squares of solid fabric. Using small slipstitches, appliqué the four pieces of the fan section to the corner of the square.

6 **To make the pincushion:** Place the two squares right sides together, and machine stitch around the outer edges, taking a seam allowance of ¼ inch and leaving a gap of 2½ inches on one side. Trim the corners and turn right side out. Stuff firmly and overstitch the gap by hand.

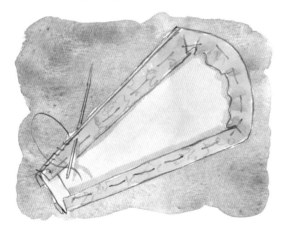

3 Press all the pieces to finish the edges, then whipstitch the fan segments together. Carefully remove basting stitches and the paper from each section.

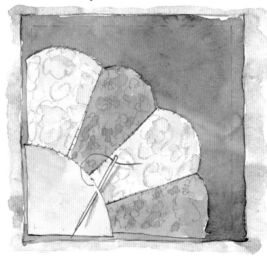

5 Remove the basting and paper from the corner piece and position it over the fan section. Appliqué in place.

7 **To make the needlecase:** Place the two squares, right sides facing, and stitch down one side so that the base of the fan motif is in the lower right-hand corner of the front. Press the seam open.

10 Make a tassel by wrapping embroidery thread around a piece of cardboard 3 inches deep. Slide the threads off, wrap another piece of thread around the top, trim the bottom and stitch to the corner of the fan motif.

8 With right sides facing, pin and baste the lining fabric and outside of the case together. Stitch the two pieces together, with a ¼-inch seam allowance and leaving a gap of 3½ inches on one side. Clip corners and seams and turn right side out. Press and topstitch all four sides, closing the gap as you do so.

9 Use pinking shears to trim the two pieces of felt to fit inside the case and stitch them in place down the center.

"QUILLOW" OR LAP QUILT

Finished size: 43 x 55 inches

When it is not being used, this lap quilt can be folded away and tucked into a matching pocket stitched to the back, so that it can do double-duty as a cushion or pillow. The patchwork top is made from two easy designs – Churn Dash and Ohio Star – which work well together. A thick batting has been used for extra warmth, and the three layers are tie-quilted.

1 Trace and make templates on page 47. Follow the cutting instructions listed on page 47. Do not cut the borders until you have finished stitching the blocks so you can be sure the length fits.

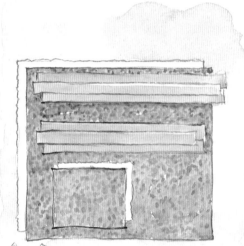

YOU WILL NEED

- needle, threads to match, pins, scissors
- purple print: 1⅝ yards
- green print: ¾ yard
- yellow print: 1¼ yards
- beige print: ¾ yard
- medium-weight polyester batting: 46 x 58 inches
- lightweight polyester batting: 19 x 19 inches
- backing: 1¾ yards (use material 60-inches wide or join pieces together)
- pearl cotton no. 8, in matching or contrasting color

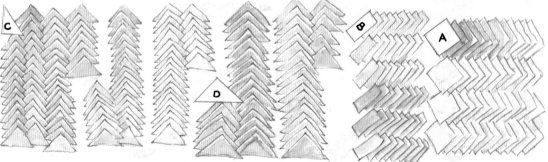

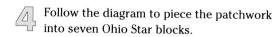

2 The patchwork top is made of 12 blocks; the pillow panel on the back requires one block. You will need six Churn Dash blocks and seven Ohio Star blocks.

Churn Dash Block

Ohio Star Block

3 Follow the diagram to piece the patchwork into six Churn Dash blocks.

4 Follow the diagram to piece the patchwork into seven Ohio Star blocks.

5 Stitch the blocks alternately together into a 3 x 4 panel. Retain one Ohio Star block for the pillow.

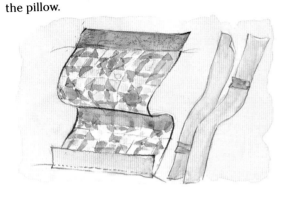

6 **Adding the borders.** Cut strips of purple fabric, 4½ inches wide, to edge the panel, stitching top and bottom first and joining strips as necessary for the sides. Press well.

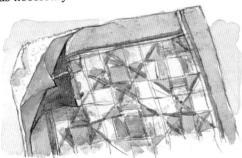

7 Place the patchwork and backing, right sides together, on top of the medium-weight batting with wrong side of patchwork on the top. Smooth and baste the three layers together around the outside edge. The backing and batting will extend beyond the patchwork. Machine stitch, taking a ¼-inch seam allowance on the patchwork and leaving a gap in one long side. Trim the excess batting and backing on all sides and corners and turn right side out.

8 Push the corners out with a knitting needle. Baste around the edges, making sure the seams lie neatly. Close the gap, then machine stitch ¼ inch from the edge.

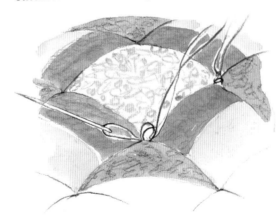

9 Thread a needle with a long strand of pearl cotton and pull it double. Make a stitch through all layers of the quilt, leaving a tail, then make a backstitch over the first and bring the needle out on the same side of the fabric. Tie the ends in a square knot, then trim to about 1inch long. Alternatively, use French knots, buttons, or beads instead of, or in addition to, the knots.

10 Make the pocket by cutting from the border fabric two strips 3 x 12½ inches, and two strips, each 3 x 17½ inches. Stitch the two shorter strips to opposite sides of the remaining Ohio Star block, then add the two longer strips to make a square 17½ x 17½ inches.

11 Cut a piece of backing fabric, 18½ x 18½ inches, and place the block and the backing right sides together on top of the lightweight batting, with the wrong side of the patchwork upward. Pin and baste the layers together. Stitch around the edges, with a ¼-inch seam allowance on the patchwork and leaving a gap on one long side. Trim the backing and batting and clip the corners, then turn right side out.

12 Push out the corners, baste around the edge, making sure the seams are straight, and close the gap. Machine stitch ¼ inch around the edge.

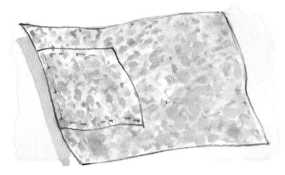

13 Position the pocket on the back of the quilt, pinning it with the patchwork side inward. Slipstitch around three sides, reinforcing the corners of the open side with extra stitches.

Make the quilt into a pillow by making two lengthwise folds in line with the sides of the pocket. Turn the pocket to the outside, pulling the bottom part of the quilt as you do so, pushing out the corners. Fold down the top end of the quilt to the edge of the pocket and tuck it inside.

FLYING GEESE STORAGE TUBE

Finished size: 10 x 24 inches

Keep your plastic bags neat and handy *with this ingenious tube. You simply push the bags in the top, then pull them out through the elasticized base when you need them.*

YOU WILL NEED

- needle, threads to match, pins, scissors
- cardboard or plastic for templates
- main fabric: ⅞ yard
- contrasting fabric: ⅜ yard
- shirring elastic: 6 inches

1 Trace and make the templates on page 47 from cardboard or plastic. Follow cutting instructions listed on page 47. Note the direction of the grain.

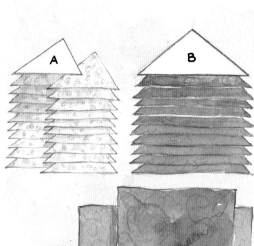

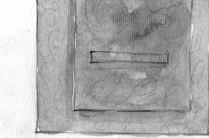

2 Piece together the patchwork panel from the triangles, taking ¼-inch seam allowance throughout. Press seams open.

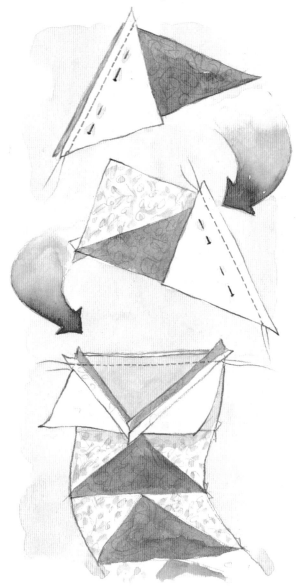

3 From the main fabric cut 1 piece 8 x 20½ inches and 1 piece 20½ x 26 inches. Stitch the patchwork panel between these two pieces. Turn, press, and stitch a narrow hem along both remaining short ends.

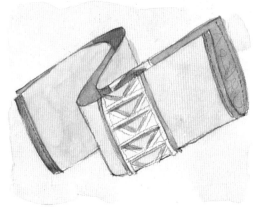

4 Fold the piece in half lengthwise, right sides together, and matching the patchwork panel. Pin and baste, then stitch the long sides together to make a tube.

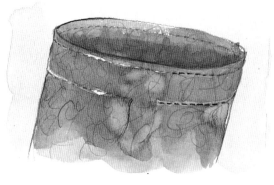

5 Turn the tube in half, with the short ends aligned and with wrong sides facing. The larger piece of fabric (the cuff and lining) should be on the inside. Pin the two open ends together matching the seams.

Make a casing for the elastic by stitching around the bottom 1 inch from the edge, then again ¼ inch in, leaving a gap in the second row through which you can thread the elastic. Pull the elastic tight, knot it, trim the ends and close the gap with a few stitches.

6 Smooth the tube so that the lining and
outer fabric lie neatly together. Topstitch
around the fold and attach a 10-inch long
hanging loop (see page 9), made in the outer
fabric, near the seam.

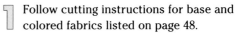

WALL POCKETS

Finished size: 21 x 27 inches

These *useful wall pockets, decorated with bright colored triangles, will provide extra storage space for a host of everyday items – string, scissors, note-pad, pens, and pencils.*

YOU WILL NEED

- needle, threads to match, pins, scissors
- base fabric: 2¼ yards
- lining: 2¼ yards
- lightweight batting: 22 x 28 inches
- colored fabrics: a total of ⅝ yard in different solid colors for the strips and triangles
- firm muslin: ⅝ yard
- hanging rod

1 Follow cutting instructions for base and colored fabrics listed on page 48.

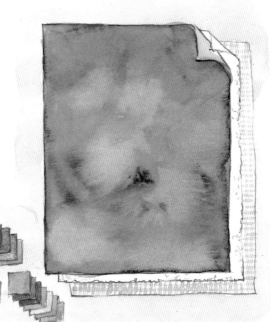

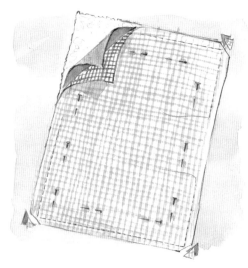

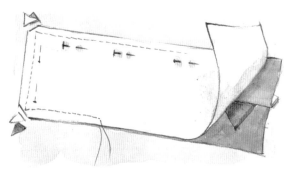

2 Baste the base fabric and lining right sides facing, with wadding underneath. Stitch ½in/1.25cm from the edge, leaving a 6in/15cm gap on one side. Trim seams and turn to the right side. Top stitch ¼in/5mm from the edge, closing the gap as you do.

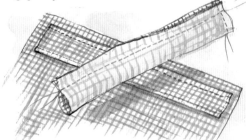

3 Fold the base fabric strip in half, right sides together, and stitch along the long edge. Press the seam open in the centre of the tube. Stitch across one short end. Turn to right side and neaten the other short end. With the seam underneath, stitch to the top of the base along the long edges, leaving the short ends open to accommodate a hanging rod.

4 Fold and press 12 colored squares in half and in half again diagonally. Make the lower pocket by marking one contrasting color strip into thirds, then arranging six triangles, in three groups of two along one edge. Make the top pocket by arranging the remaining triangles in two sets of three. Place the second contrasting strip, right side down, over the first strip. Stitch together, trapping the triangles in the seam. Topstitch on front.

5 Place the pockets, right sides down, on the muslin and cut lining to match. Stitch the pockets to the lining, leaving a gap on the lower edge. Trim and turn right side out. Press.

6 Make the center pockets in the same way as the lower and top, but cut strips 3 x 13 inches for the left-hand pocket and 3 x 6 inches for the right-hand pocket. Position seven more triangles.

7 Make a loop, for scissors, from a strip of fabric 2 x 6 inches (see page 9).

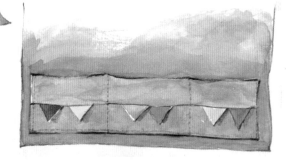

8 Position the lower pockets along the bottom of the base and stitch around the sides and bottom edge. Divide the pocket in three and stitch the vertical lines.

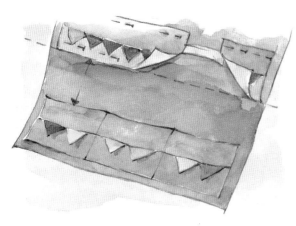

9 Draw a line on the base, 5 inches above the lower pockets. Position the center pockets on this line, with the scissor loop between them and under the sides of the pockets. Stitch sides and bottom edges.

10 Work a buttonhole to hold string on one side of the top pockets. Position the top pockets 3 inches from the top edge. Stitch sides and bottom edges, divide into three and stitch vertical lines, making a narrow section for pens and pencils.

Trim all ends and insert the hanging rod.

BELT OR SHOULDER PURSE

Finished size: 7 x 8 inches

When you are traveling, this is the ideal way to keep your passport and other valuables safe. The purse will fit onto a belt or you can thread a length of cord through the side loops for a shoulder strap.

YOU WILL NEED

- needle, threads to match, pins, scissors
- scraps of pattern fabric for patchwork panel: 19 pieces, each 1½ x 3½ inches
- paper for templates
- fabric for side panels: ¼ yard
- lining fabric: ¼ yard
- iron-on interfacing: 8 x 19 inches
- snap fastener

1 Trace and make templates on page 48 from cardboard or plastic. Follow the cutting instructions listed on page 48.

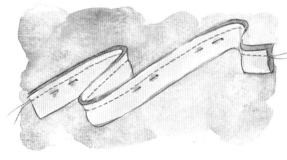

3 Iron the interfacing to the wrong side of the patchwork piece.

4 Make the side loop by folding the strip of fabric in half lengthwise, right sides together, and stitch the long edge. Trim seam and turn right side out. Press the seam at center back.

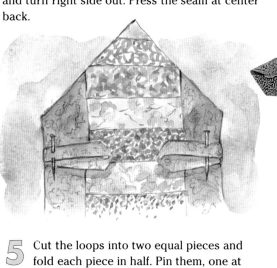

7 Fold up the bottom 7 inches and baste the sides together to form a square. Stitch the two sides, closing the gap and creating a pocket. Sew on the snap to close the purse.

5 Cut the loops into two equal pieces and fold each piece in half. Pin them, one at each side, to the edge of the patchwork piece.

6 Place the patchwork and lining together, right sides facing. Stitch around the outer edge, trapping the loops in the stitching, but leaving a gap on one of the long sides. Trim the seam and turn right side out. Press.

2 Stitch 19 patchwork pieces in a long strip, taking a ¼-inch seam allowance. Press seams to one side. Stitch two side panels, right sides facing, aligning the straight ends with the bottom of the strip. Press seams to the side. Topstitch on side panels ¼ inch from seam.

CRAZY PATCHWORK WALL HANGING

Finished size: 31 x 38 inches

Crazy patchwork is an excellent method of using up scraps of fabric. It was especially popular in the 19th century, when all kinds of exotic materials, left over from elaborate dresses, were used, together with scraps of ribbon, lace, embroidered details, and even sentimental mementoes. This wall hanging is made from 12 individual blocks, with linking strips in the single color. Although the scraps are irregular shapes, they should all have straight sides.

1 Follow the cutting instructions on page 48. Do not cut the border strips until you have completed the block to be sure they fit.

YOU WILL NEED

- needle, threads to match, pins, scissors
- scraps of silk, taffeta, satin, etc.
- medium-weight muslin: 1¼ yards
- embroidery thread
- sashing: ⅝ yard
- solid cotton for border: ⅝ yard
- backing fabric: 1¼ yards
- lightweight polyester batting: 1¼ yards
- black binding fabric: ⅝ yard

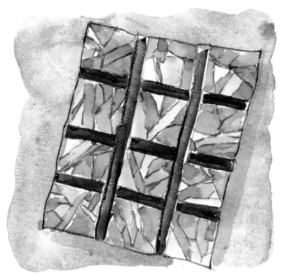

2 Place a 4- or 5-sided scrap of fabric in the corner of a muslin square, right side up. Press and pin. Following the diagram, place a second scrap over the first, right sides together, aligning one straight edge. Stitch through both layers of silk and muslin. Press and unfold the second piece. Trim the sides so the straight edge of the first patch extends along the second. Continue in this way, varying the shapes and sizes of the patches, until you have completed 12 large and 4 small squares. Trim the blocks to square them up and baste around the edges to fasten the scraps to the muslin. Embroider the seams with a linear stitch, such as herringbone, feather stitch or fly stitch.

4 Use the two longer strips of sashing to join the three strips. Trim all edges.

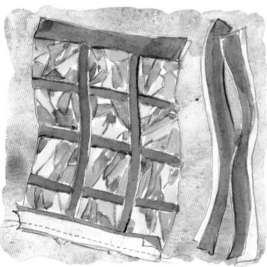

3 Back the sashing with muslin so it is a similar weight to the blocks. Use the short sashing strips to join the large squares in three rows of four squares each.

5 Adding the inner border: Measure the length of the finished work and cut four border strips in sashing 2 inches wide. Back with muslin. Stitch pieces in position.

43

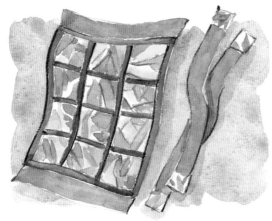

8 Cut strips of binding 2½ inches wide, joining as necessary to make a strip long enough to go right around the finished work. Fold in half lengthwise and press. Stitch to the right side of the patchwork, miter the corners (see page 9). Turn the binding to the back and hem by hand. To accommodate a hanging rod, follow Step 3 on page 38 (Wall Pockets).

6 Adding the outer border: Again check the correct lengths of the finished work, and cut four strips 4 inches wide. Stitch the longer sides first. Stitch the small patchwork squares to each end of the shorter border strips, then add the shorter border strips, top and bottom. Topstitch the outer edge of the border

7 Make a sandwich of the backing fabric, batting, and the finished patchwork and pin and baste in horizontal and vertical rows at intervals of 6 inches. Quilt around each block and each border piece by machine or by hand. Remove basting stitches.

TEMPLATES

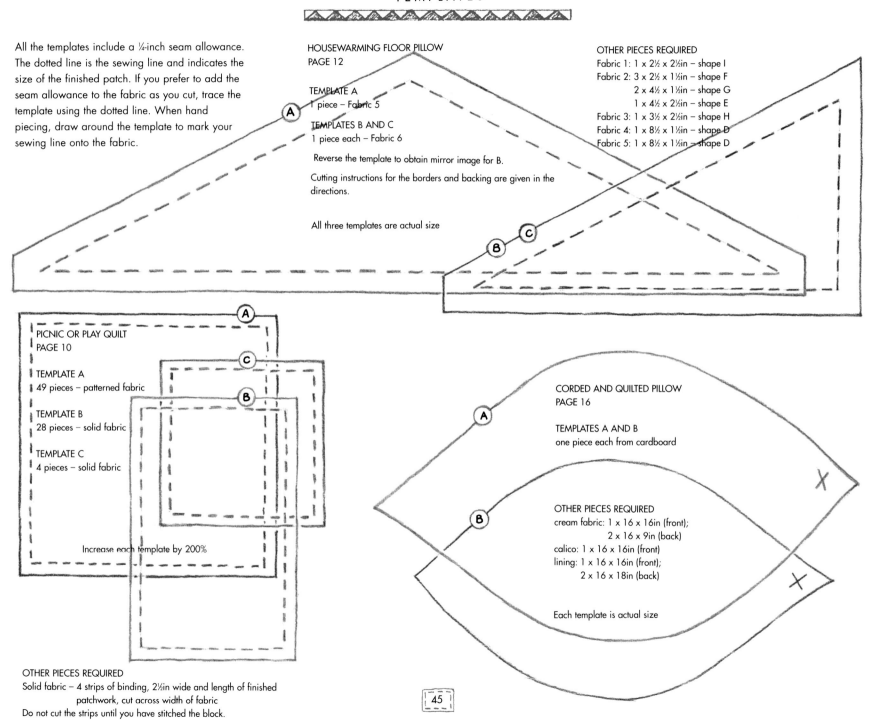

All the templates include a ¼-inch seam allowance. The dotted line is the sewing line and indicates the size of the finished patch. If you prefer to add the seam allowance to the fabric as you cut, trace the template using the dotted line. When hand piecing, draw around the template to mark your sewing line onto the fabric.

HOUSEWARMING FLOOR PILLOW
PAGE 12

TEMPLATE A
1 piece – Fabric 5

TEMPLATES B AND C
1 piece each – Fabric 6

Reverse the template to obtain mirror image for B.

Cutting instructions for the borders and backing are given in the directions.

All three templates are actual size

OTHER PIECES REQUIRED
Fabric 1: 1 x 2½ x 2½in – shape I
Fabric 2: 3 x 2½ x 1½in – shape F
2 x 4½ x 1½in – shape G
1 x 4½ x 2½in – shape E
Fabric 3: 1 x 3½ x 2½in – shape H
Fabric 4: 1 x 8½ x 1½in – shape D
Fabric 5: 1 x 8½ x 1½in – shape D

PICNIC OR PLAY QUILT
PAGE 10

TEMPLATE A
49 pieces – patterned fabric

TEMPLATE B
28 pieces – solid fabric

TEMPLATE C
4 pieces – solid fabric

Increase each template by 200%

OTHER PIECES REQUIRED
Solid fabric – 4 strips of binding, 2½in wide and length of finished patchwork, cut across width of fabric
Do not cut the strips until you have stitched the block.

CORDED AND QUILTED PILLOW
PAGE 16

TEMPLATES A AND B
one piece each from cardboard

OTHER PIECES REQUIRED
cream fabric: 1 x 16 x 16in (front);
2 x 16 x 9in (back)
calico: 1 x 16 x 16in (front)
lining: 1 x 16 x 16in (front);
2 x 16 x 18in (back)

Each template is actual size

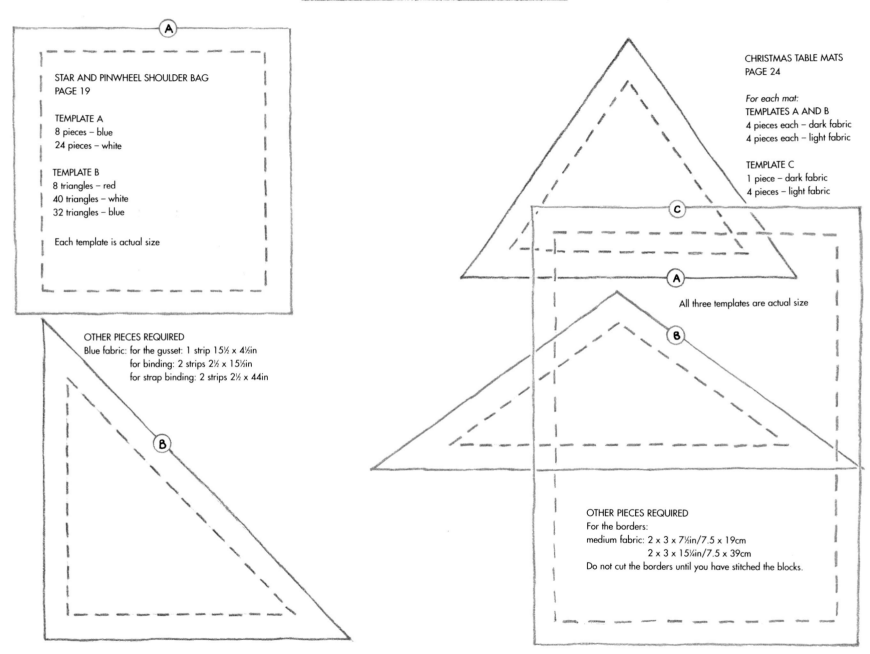

STAR AND PINWHEEL SHOULDER BAG
PAGE 19

TEMPLATE A
8 pieces – blue
24 pieces – white

TEMPLATE B
8 triangles – red
40 triangles – white
32 triangles – blue

Each template is actual size

OTHER PIECES REQUIRED
Blue fabric: for the gusset: 1 strip 15½ x 4½in
for binding: 2 strips 2½ x 15½in
for strap binding: 2 strips 2½ x 44in

CHRISTMAS TABLE MATS
PAGE 24

For each mat:
TEMPLATES A AND B
4 pieces each – dark fabric
4 pieces each – light fabric

TEMPLATE C
1 piece – dark fabric
4 pieces – light fabric

All three templates are actual size

OTHER PIECES REQUIRED
For the borders:
medium fabric: 2 x 3 x 7½in/7.5 x 19cm
2 x 3 x 15¼in/7.5 x 39cm
Do not cut the borders until you have stitched the blocks.

FAN MOTIF PINCUSHION AND NEEDLECASE PAGE 27

cardboard

fabric

FOR EACH ITEM:
TEMPLATE A
4 pieces – patterned fabric

TEMPLATE B
1 pieces – patterned fabric

Each template
is actual size

cardboard

fabric

OTHER PIECES REQUIRED
Plain fabric: 2 x 4½ x 4½in
Interfacing: 2 x 4½ x 4½in
Lining fabric for needlecase: 4½ x 10in

QUILLOW OR LAP QUILT PAGE 30

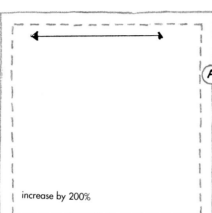

increase by 200%

increase by 200%

FLYING GEESE STORAGE TUBE PAGE 34

TEMPLATE A
20 pieces – contrasting fabric

TEMPLATE B
10 pieces – main fabric

OTHER PIECES REQUIRED
in main fabric:
1 x 20½ x 18in/52 x 46cm
1 x 20½ x 26in/52 x 66cm

Increase each template by 133%

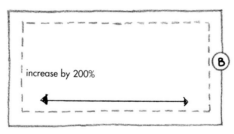

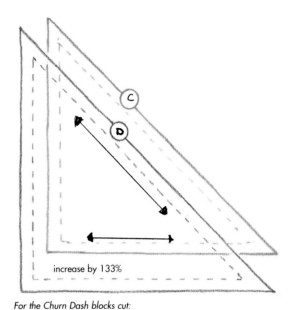

increase by 133%

For the Churn Dash blocks cut:
Template A: 6 pieces – yellow
Template B: 24 pieces – green; 24 pieces – beige
Template C: 24 pieces – purple; 24 pieces – beige

For the Ohio Star blocks cut:
Template A: 7 pieces – purple; 28 pieces – yellow
Template D: 56 pieces – purple; 28 pieces – green;
28 pieces – yellow

Cutting instructions for the borders are given in the directions. Do not cut the borders until you have stitched the blocks.

Note the direction of the grain.

TEMPLATES

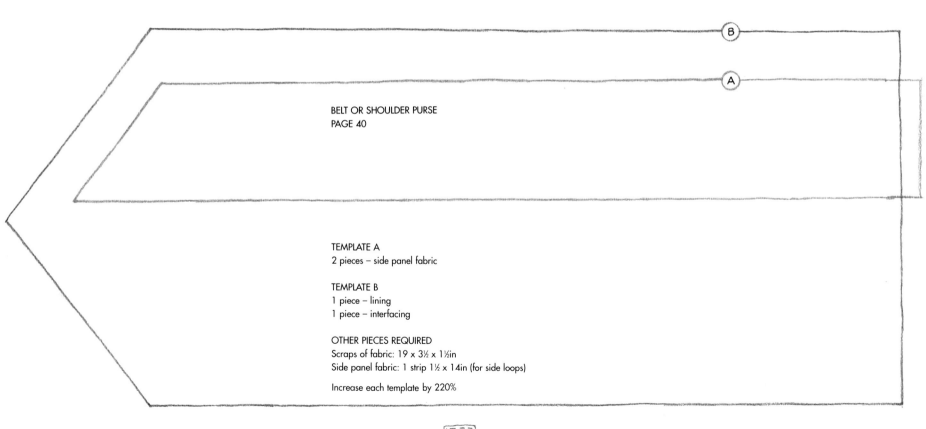

CRAZY PATCHWORK WALL-HANGING
PAGE 42

PIECES REQUIRED
muslin: 12 squares 7 x 7in
4 squares 4 x 4in
1 x 18 x 36in (optional)
sashing: 9 x 7 x 2in
2 x 32 x 2in
inner border: 2 x 21½ x 2in
2 x 31½ x 2in
outer border: 2 x 27 x 4in
2 x 34 x 4in
binding fabric: 1 x 18 x 36in
Do not cut the borders until you have stitched the block.

WALL POCKETS
PAGE 37

PIECES REQUIRED
Base fabric: 1 rectangle: 21½ x 27½in
1 strip: 22 x 6in
1 strip: 2 x 6in (for scissor loop)
Lining: 1 rectangle: 21½ x 27½in
Colored fabrics: 19 squares: 3 x 3in
4 strips: 21 x 3in
2 strips: 13 x 3in
2 strips: 6 x 3in

BELT OR SHOULDER PURSE
PAGE 40

TEMPLATE A
2 pieces – side panel fabric

TEMPLATE B
1 piece – lining
1 piece – interfacing

OTHER PIECES REQUIRED
Scraps of fabric: 19 x 3½ x 1½in
Side panel fabric: 1 strip 1½ x 14in (for side loops)

Increase each template by 220%